AF604284

First published by Allen & Unwin in 2025

Allen & Unwin
Cammeraygal Country
83 Alexander Street
Crows Nest NSW 2065
Australia
Phone: (61 2) 8425 0100
Email: info@allenandunwin.com
Web: www.allenandunwin.com

Allen & Unwin acknowledges the Traditional Owners of the Country on which we live and work.We pay our respects to all Aboriginal and Torres Strait Islander Elders, past and present.

EU Authorised Representative: Easy Access System Europe, Mustamäe tee 50, 10621 Tallinn, Estonia, gpsr.requests@easproject.com

A catalogue record for this book is available from the National Library of Australia

ISBN 978 1 76118 220 4

For teaching resources, explore allenandunwin.com/learn

Illustration technique: hand-drawn using Procreate

Cover and text design by Joanna Hunt
Set in 20pt Quicksand Medium
This book was printed in April 2025 in China by Hang Tai Printing Company Limited.

1 2 3 4 5 6 7 8 9 10

mitchtambo.com
carlahoffenberg.com

Phoenix, Kalani, Sofiana, Ofa
Never forget how loved you are.

To my beautiful wife Voice of Lele,
thank you for your unwavering
support and unconditional love.
I love you my queen.

I acknowledge Aunty Bernadette
Duncan, Buddy Hippi and all of my
culture teachers along my journey.

All the language and knowledge
shared in this book is from
Gamilaraay Country. **MT**

To Ty, Cody and Mason
May you always be proud of
who you are, build bridges
and help make the world
a better place. **CH**

I AM ME

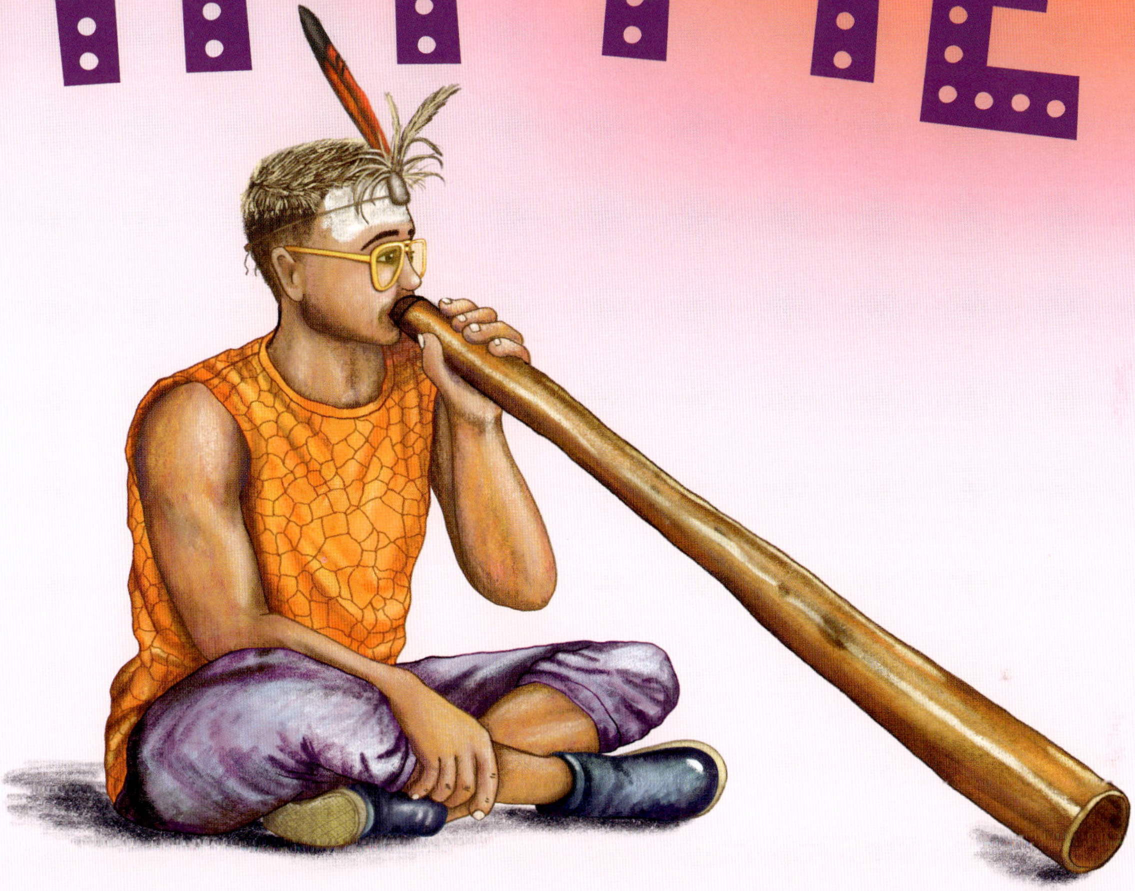

MITCH TAMBO

Illustrated by CARLA HOFFENBERG

Yaama!

My name is **Mitch Tambo**.

What's your name?

I'm a proud First Nations man who grew up on Gamilaraay Country and was raised within the Gamilaraay culture.

I'm also proud to be a Biripi and Worimi man learning about my connections to my culture, peoples and family.

Who are your people?

In my language, to say **Hello** we say **Yaama**.

I like to give big hellos so I say, **Yaama Yaama!**

How do you say Hello in your language?

I love to sing in my Gamilaraay language

and I love to dance.

In Gamilaraay language we say **Yugal** for **Sing** and **Yulu-gi** for **Dance**.

What do you say in your language?

I would like to acknowledge
the First Nations land
that you live on and play
on with your friends.

Do you know the name
of the First Nations land
you are on?

Dhirribuu!

This is our way of saying

Great job.

I love to wear my sacred headdress
whenever I perform.

In my headdress I wear a **Bilirr**,
a Red-Tailed Black Cockatoo feather.

This honours the story of Bilirr bringing us fire and also represents keeping the fire burning – keeping my culture alive.

Can you see the fire in the feather of Bilirr?

Is there anything you do to keep your culture alive?

Do you do special dances or wear special things?

Do you have special songs or stories, or eat extra-yummy food?

The next feathers in my headdress are from **Dhinawan**.

In my language, this is the word for **Emu**.

Did you know that Dhinawan can only walk forwards, not backwards?

Dhinawan teaches us that we should always walk forwards and never give up, even when times get tough.

We can see the shape of Dhinawan in the Milky Way.

Have you ever seen the Milky Way?

It's a beautiful group of stars in the sky.

We call the Milky Way **Warrambul**.

Can you see the glue holding my feathers together?

What do you think it's made of?

Well, it's wax from our native honeybee.

We get its wax and melt it.

We add ashes from the campfire which make it into a glue.

Last but not least, can you see the paint on my forehead?

What colour is it?

Yes, it is white.

Dhirribuu!

This paint is called **ochre**.

Ochre is made from a special rock that we collect.

We crush it into powder and mix it with water.

Then our ochre turns into a beautiful paint that we can use on our bodies to tell our stories.

We also use it in our paintings.

Ochre comes in many different colours,
like red, yellow and white.

What's your favourite colour?

Mine is purple.

Once I’ve painted my forehead and put on my headdress it’s nearly time to sing and dance.

But first I have to find my favourite sparkly shirt and my favourite glasses . . .

Ahh . . . that's better!

Do you have a favourite outfit you wear when you sing and dance?

Quick, go put it on!

Now it's time to sing and dance . . . **Wahooooo!**

Guwaa-li Yilaa!

Talk soon!

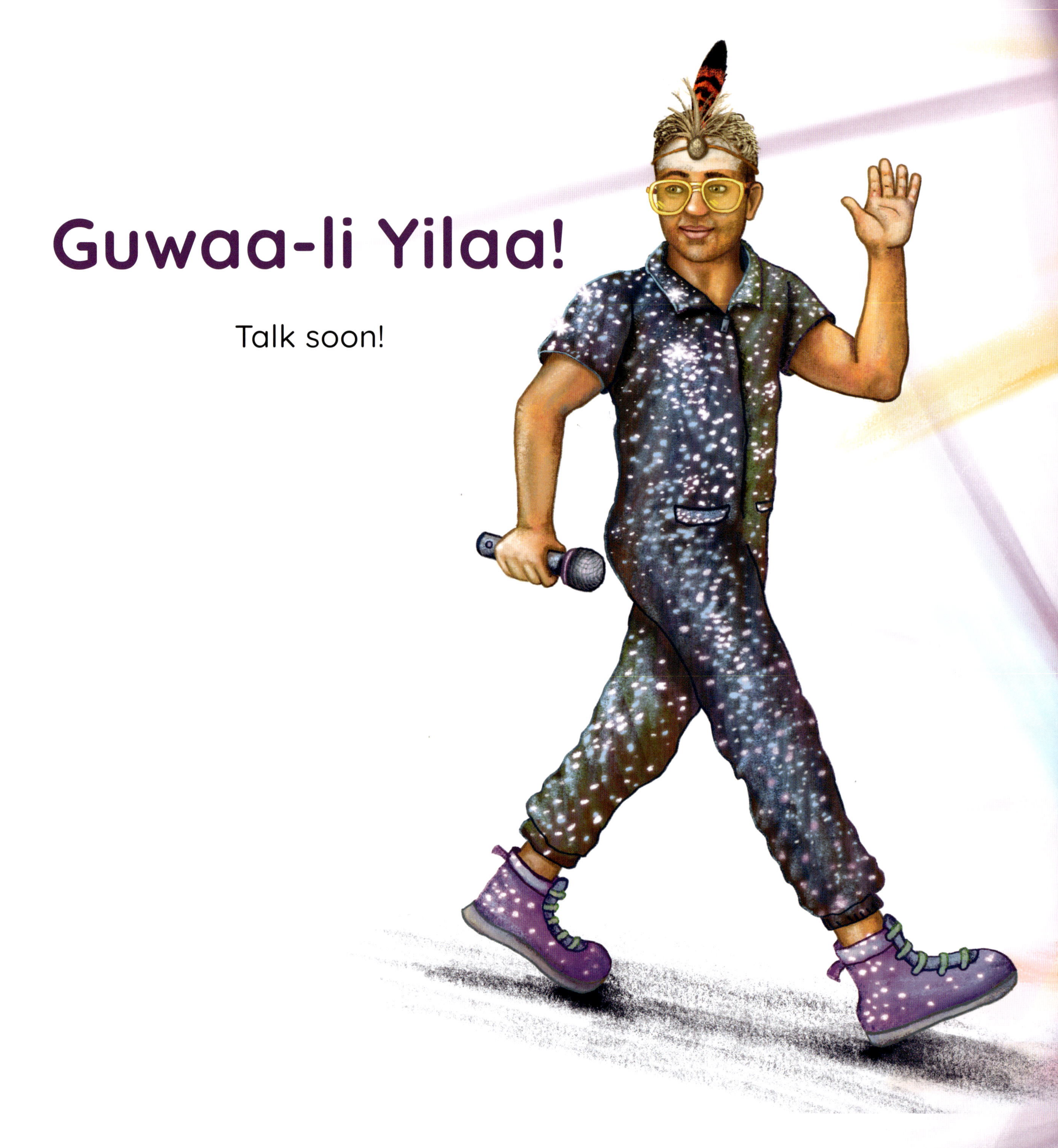

Thank you so much for reading my book and learning about my culture.

I hope one day I can come to your school and share my songs with you all.

Until then you can sing and dance with me on TikTok, Facebook, Instagram and YouTube!